Somersaults On Mattresses

By Wycla Bratton

ISBN: 979-8-9856197-6-8

Cover design: Avenue K Web Design

Printed in the United States of America

Robinson Anderson Publishing
2150 South Central Expressway, Suite 200
McKinney, TX 75070
info@rapublishingco.com

To the person reading this book,
you are loved.

Contents

Project

– noun

1. *something that is contemplated, devised, or planned; plan; scheme.*
2. *the projects, ... a housing project*

(dictionary.com)

Sight and Vision

If you're from the projects
you can't afford to not be
optimistic.

The way that it's intended
you won't get it
if you're a realist.

Become what you see
or become what you see.

d e v i s e d

P
L
A
N
N
E
D

scheme

Devised

verb

past tense: **devised**; *past participle*: **devised**

1. plan or invent (a complex procedure, system, or mechanism) by careful thought.

(Oxford Languages)

History Lesson Part 1

Patriots

> *George Washington*
> *Thomas Jefferson*
> *Alexander Hamilton*
> *Benjamin Franklin*

Psych Mike Says...

What are you looking for?

God gave you everything you need.

Home

Youngins influencin'
the world again.

Gymnast on mattresses,
somersaults and back bends.

Fashion models'
unorthodox struts.

Vibrations from box chevys,
heartbeats in the trunk.

Businessmen who deal
in hand-to-hand transactions.

The neighborhood's grandma,
Knower of all.

Cars on chrome, daytons, and hubcaps.
Foreigners with shiny badges and guns.

Smiles from the neighbors,
the young old, and the old young.

The Highway

runs right through
the side of town
our grandparents
used to live.

On Every Corner

there's a store that sells genies
who work part time.

Psych Mike

was always selling random things.

"Look what I got; I know you could use something."

From the bag of THANK YOU
spoils fell on the porch in a crescendo:
AA battery
Can of corn
Pleather jacket
Rope
Lighter—

that wasn't for sale.

Flashlight
Hair tie
Bandana
Rings
Glass tube—

that also wasn't for sale.

The Water Park

Every neighborhood has one,

someone just has to open it.

Lucky for us,

TJ's dad was the manager.

The fun lasts

until the firemen come.

The Candy Store

No shopping carts.
No aisles.
No angry cashier.
No tax.

A table in the kitchen,
maybe the living room.

A dime was not too little.
A dollar was not too much.

Just a lady in a chair
smiling.

"Hey babies, whatchall want?"

Box Chevy Parade

Box chariots could be heard
from far and wide.

We raced to see them
in slow motion.

Bright colors.

Shiny spokes.

Stars in our eyes
as they rode by.

Psych Mike Says...

People judge me but
if they'd mind their own
they'd see
I'm not the only one
with an addiction.

Close Relatives

I've seen so many roaches
I think I can tell them apart
we're practically cousins.

Mama's Grocery List:

Bologna

Crackers

Ketchup

Mustard

Tuna

Eggs

Milk

Juice

Bread

Spam

Yes

Spam

Chips

from Royal Liquor...

and bring her change back, all of it.

Styling My Crown

Orange can

90 strokes to the front
90 strokes to the right
90 strokes to the back
90 strokes to the left

Stocking cap

First Day of School

Uniform shirt   Crispy
Pants   Dickies
Shoes

Jokes dressed me
in a large 'fro,
white face,
red nose.

My FUBUs stretched
with every sluggish minute,
becoming more apparent with every joke.

When the bell rang,
I prepared for an encore
in the hallway...

"Aye homie, we was just messin' with you.
You hoop?
Bet, come to the blacktop at lunch...

you still wrong for wearing those shoes though!"

My Homies

My Boys

My Gs

My Dawgs

My Guys

My Mans

My Potnas

My Friends

My Hittas

My Brothas

My Folks

My Bros

We Went to The Same School

Ate in each other's homes.
Shared the same clothes.

No one tells you these are your friends.

The same way no one tells you to breathe.

Malik

Jay

Flip

Me

Malik

Protector

Focused

Taciturn

Respected

Prudent

Organized

Decisive

Humble

Disciplined

Aware

Jay

The only child
of a single mom.

His dad
was last seen
this past summer

on the news

and t-shirts.

Flip

The youngest of 3 boys
from a family of flippers

stars of the 4 square circus.

He never wanted for anything
made sure we were good too.

Forever Living In Prosperity

Me

Mom and Pop's first child.
First of many
mistakes
and successes.

I hadn't spent much time
in their presence

but, I have a desire
to do well in life.
Just don't know how yet.

Psych Mike Says...

The smaller your circle

the easier it is to get around.

Planned

verb

past tense: planned; past partici¹ple: planned

      1. decide on and arrange in advance.

      2. design or make a plan of (something to

        be ***made or built).***

(Oxford *Languages)*

Today's History Lesson Pt. 2

Rebels

    Booker T. Washington

    Marcus Garvey

    Martin Luther King Jr.

    Malcolm X

Psych Mike Says...

The war on drugs.
The war on terror.
The war on our minds.

Ima Be A Rapper!

They gone call me Jay Money
best believe Ima have all the honeys!
Shoot, that's a bar right there!

Ha! Shut up foo.
I'm going to the NBA
the announcer gone be like
"Wearing number four
Kairooooooooooooooooooo!"

What... What I want to be?
I'm already getting this money.

I will be an English teacher.

We Never Saw A Black Dude Teach Anything

outside of PE
or that one class,
where it's a few kids.

Mom said teachers don't make a lot of money.

Didn't seem to bother Malik though.

My teacher told me I wasn't like them

Flip
Jay

"You mean my hom—"
"Your friends Kairo, you can speak better than that."

I felt strange.

How could I not be like them?
We come from the same place,

talk the same
walk the same
look the same.

So if I wasn't like them

who was I like?

Aye, Where You From?

Westside Motherland,
Gold Coast.

The landmark of wealth.
That territory of shackles.

Chained ankles, wrist and minds
but not the spirit.
The spirit lives
and through us they live.

So we could pass the message
that we, are not alone
that we, are powerful
that abundance, is our birthright.

It is not ourselves we are to fight

but instead, I tell him

I don't bang.

Lesson Learned

Before that, I got jumped.

Before that, I received threats.

Before that, I thought everything was sweet.

Before that, I pushed a dude in the hallway.

Before that, we all planned to push someone.

Before that, we came up with this plan to be cool.

Before that, I just wanted to be cool.

Before that, Mama said "Don't go up there acting a
    fool."

Before that, Mama said "Don't be trying to impress no
    little girl."

Before that, Mama said "All you have to do is be
    yourself."

I Didn't Know The Answer

If I asked, I would look dumb
I couldn't risk looking dumb.

I didn't know the answer
I couldn't risk being clowned.

I didn't know the answer
too much embarrassment.

I didn't know the answer
Hakim didn't neither.

Hakim didn't care about looking dumb
Hakim couldn't risk not knowing.

Hakim always asked
Hakim could risk being clowned.

Hakim always asked
it wasn't embarrassing.

Hakim always asked
Hakim always got an answer.

Psych Mike Says...

Don't look down on me.

I may not look like I have much
but I have joy.

Scheme
noun

1.

BRITISH

a large-scale systematic plan or arrangement for attaining a particular object or putting a particular idea into effect.

2.

INFORMAL•SCOTTISH

a public housing complex.

verb

1. *make plans, especially in a devious way or with intent to do something illegal or wrong.*

(Oxford Languages)

Today's History Lesson Pt. 3

Independent Research

        Angela Davis

        Assata Shakur

        Claudette Colvin

        Fannie Lou Hamer

Psych Mike Says...

You

Attract

You

Malia

I didn't know you could freeze time.
I was astonished by your beauty.
I heard English was your favorite subject so
I hope this is good enough.

I thought I knew what beautiful was
then I was allured by your conspicuous elegance.

Is it possible to impress
someone of eminence?

I guess what I'm asking is...

Do you like me?

Yes ☐
No ☐

Psych Mike says...

Youngblood!
Lemme hold sum,
c'mon now baby
it's me.

Psych Mike and Flip

Caught in the trap.
They need each other.
Perhaps they'd do better
without each other.

Psych Mike Says...

Rappers must have signed a contract
that said
you can rap about killing folk
but everything else
that's off limits.

Roman Candles

We used to light them
aim at the sky
and shake 'til empty.
Somewhere down the line
we started pointing them
at each other.

The Sub

Mr. Howard asked us what we would do if he gave us $1,000.

"I'm getting the 1s, 4s, and 11s"
"I might have to get that Gucci belt"

"IDK my guy"
"Grabbing some new Tims, the wheats of course."
"Get an Xbox!"
"Xbox trash bruh"

"That's cap"
"That ain't even a lot of money"
"Right, what's a baller like me going to do with $1,000"

"Free money is free money my nigga"
"Watch it."
"My bad Mr. Howard"

"Your responses are interesting, not to shade y'all but that's one of our problems."
"What you trying to say Mr., we can't want nice things?"

"Nope, not at all. You should desire to have nice things, but what if we were able to accumulate more money before we got those nice things?"

"I mean, that sounds cool and all but..."

"Check this out, everyone write this down on a piece of paper... The Power of Compounding..."

I liked Mr. Howard, he was cool.

Psych Mike says...

Back in my day
we used to go outside and play.

When *we had disagreements*
we got rounds
and went about our day.

You *youngbloods have*
disagreements catch rounds
and make the news.

The Human Zoo

A few times a month

suits, dresses,

hard bottoms and heels

come to watch us

like animals in an unnatural

habitat. A zoo.

We don't get the luxury

of being cheered on

to show what we can do.

They stare

write on their pads

and leave

remembering to close the door.

HANDS ON YOUR HEAD NOW!!!!!!!!!!!!!!!!!!!!!

I tried to shrink

so

small

to be so

I n v I s I b l e

but I
kept standing out.

Maybe

I

should stop hanging

where Jay's dad made the news.

Sex Ed

It took three hours
$99.99
of pay-per-view

for me to receive my first lesson.

Dad said you do that when
you love someone
and get married.

I left that conversation believing love was physical

and that I

                was
            a mistake.

My Mama Says If We Want Something In This World

all we have to do is pray

so I asked

"Is this all you wanted?"

Perspective

I resented my parents
with everything I know
now. Why didn't they

teach me finance
read to me
come to all my games
help me be confident
help me love myself
wipe my tears away
protect me...

An endless list of
what they should have done
what I could have become.

Two teens created life
while trying to figure it out.
Wondering why they didn't
receive what they needed

Left to do
what they could
with what they knew.

Flip Wasn't Much Of A Hugger

For some reason
this day
it seemed to be
the only thing
he could say.

Psych Mike Says...

Some people don't believe in God
say they can't see Him.
Well, they can't see oxygen neither.

Absent

My dad doesn't know
I was homeless
in foster care
alone
molested.

My Uncle And I

Sat in the parking lot
in his box Chevy
waiting
watching.

Without warning
a man in his car
flew through the lot.

My uncle calmly said
you're rushing to live
you're rushing to die.

The Spot Was In The Middle of Our Community

It was only a big green block
but the vibes were electric.

Malia Used To Live a Few Blocks Away From Me

So did a lot of kids that go to my school.
One day our bus didn't stop there anymore.
The building was torn down.
A sign read *Luxury Living Coming Soon*.

They were building a better place for Malia to live.

Psych Mike Says...

Y'all youngbloods be careful out here now.

The Usual Thunderstorm

Starts off as a disagreement

most often a misunderstanding.

The sun stops shining for a while

but the storm doesn't last long.

This time
we all escaped from the rain
except for Flip.

He was struck by lightning.

The News Said

"A man was killed in a gang related altercation."

His mom said
"They took my baby."

The pastor said
"May he rest in Heaven."

Guys from the block said
"They gone get theirs."

I know
Flip
just wanted to be free.

Anger Is Like Walking Into A Field of Burs

The moment you enter the field
you have become a reflection of the environment.

In this field I stand
waiting
waiting
waiting
with the burs
for our next victim.

I chose to make sure
they would get theirs.

In my hand
a weight—
heavier than I expected.

In my mind

The weight of knowing what my mom would feel.
The weight of knowing I'd lose years of my life.

The weight of joining the four square circus.
The weight of watering the burs with the same gore.

The weight of Malik's hand
wiping the burs from me.

Psych Mike says...

You know
I had a good life
before all this.
I ruined it *all.*

A *woman gave me*
this book though
says there's still a chance.

Somersault

noun

1. an acrobatic movement in which a person turns head over ***heels in the air or on the ground and lands or finishes on their feet.***

verb

1. perform a ***somersault, or make a similar movement accidentally.***

(Oxford Languages)

Today's History Lesson Pt. 4

In The Making
>   Eric Thomas
>   Tiffany The Budgetnista
>   Christopher Emdin
>   Earn Your Leisure

We Say Aight Then

instead of goodbye

Yelling out "I see you!"
when you're fly.

On everything we love
when we're serious.

Saying the name once
could mean one person.
Saying the name twice
could be another.

What's up?
What you trying to do?
What's good?
Depends on the situation.

I love how we speak
Us
across the nation.

At School They Tell Us...

Go to college and leave
here.
Better yet, don't come back
here.
And that's why things don't change
here.

Hands of Scholars Fly in the Air

like fireworks on independence
day. Every day
scholars enter
and leave
better writers, readers, and speakers.

Steps taken now
to better forevers.
Curiosity peaks
victories won.

Smiles and Laughter.
Peace and Love.
Daps and Shakes.
Pats and Hugs.

Good mornings,
afternoons,
have a nice day
and warm replies.
"You too, Mr. Kairo."

We Grow Up

thinking
what we experienced
is what life is.

Extremities are normal.
Trauma is unnoticed
unacknowledged
ignored.

Escaping a system
structured to confine
mental confinement
is overlooked
undervalued.

We grow up
when we understand.

Our experience was
just that, an experience
that strengthens and inspires.
One that is globally
studied, copied, and broadcasted.

We grow up
when we learn

to love
where we come from
contribute to it's embetterment
time, energy
Love
Love
Love
Love.

I See Them

at their desk
hungry
for more than content.

The school only feeds them
aesthetics
filling them so much
they're not able
to express their real needs.

Contorted
Askew
Maimed
and Marred

Their urge to resist
while regurgitating
foriegn matter.

Organic substance
is needed
but isn't
the standard diet.

Organic substance
is needed
but hidden.

Organic substance is
needed
but rejected.

Organic substance
is needed
even it it means
I'm plucked
from the garden.

I Went Away

and came back
with an adjusted lens.

I don't remember it
looking like this

when I was in
the midst.

Retrospect

I ~~resented~~ understand my parents
with everything I know
now. Why ~~didn't they~~ they didn't

teach me finance
read to me
come to all my games
help me be confident
help me love myself
wipe my tears away
protect me...

An endless list of
what they ~~should~~ have done
what I ~~could have~~ am becoming.

Two teens created life
while trying to figure it out.

Wondering why they didn't
receive what they needed

Left to do
what they could
with what they knew.

Friends

Some are lifelong.
Some come and go.
Some are there to teach.
Some are there to learn.
Some say let's plan.
Some say remember when.

Psych Mike

Still on the corner
with a book now
glad to see
he seized
that chance.

Where I'm From

there's bliss

there's struggle

there's peace

there's violence

there's laughter

there's tears

there's courage

there's fear.

There's the same things
you'd find anywhere else.

The Tall Building

connected us.
The concrete
perfected us.

Shades of mahogany mocha leaves
lay away
in the breeze.

Leaves
of the baobab tree.
We
raise our crown.

Psych Mike Says...

Every day you wake up
appreciate that gift
you have purpose here.

We All Have To Start Somewhere

some have better beginnings than others.

How you start the project is not final
there are rough drafts in between.

You look at what you have so far
then you make the necessary tweaks

to create a
polished piece.

Sincerely,
A Project Kid